See How They Grow

See How Cats Grow

Kathryn Walker

PowerKiDS
press.
New York

Published in 2009 by The Rosen Publishing Group Inc.
29 East 21st Street, New York, NY 10010

First Edition

Library of Congress Cataloging-in-Publication Data

Walker, Kathryn, 1957-
  See how cats grow / Kathryn Walker. — 1st ed.
    p. cm. — (See how they grow)
  Includes index.
  ISBN 978-1-4358-2829-2 (library binding)
  ISBN 978-1-4358-2875-9 (paperback)
  ISBN 978-1-4358-2876-6 (6-pack)
  1. Cats–Development—Juvenile literature. I. Title.
  SF445.7.W35 2009
  636.8—dc22
                                    2008027166

Manufactured in China

The publishers would like to thank the following for allowing us to reproduce
their pictures in this book:
Corbis: 14 (Cecilia Enholm/Etsa), 17 (K & H Benser/zefa), 21 (Jim Craigmyle).
FLPA: cover (Konrad Wothe/ Minden Pictures), 5 (Flip de Nooyer/Foto Natura),
6 (Tony Hamblin), 9 (Angela Hampton), 15 (Mitsuaki Iwago/Minden Pictures), 19
(Photo Natura catalogue). Getty Images: 8 (Kenneth Garrett/National Geographic),
10, 11 and 16 (Jane Burton/Dorling Kindersley collection), 23 (Arthur Tilley/Taxi).
Istockphoto: title page and page 18, 4 (Justin Horrocks), 7, 12 (Mark Hayes), 13
(Alberto Perez Veiga), 20 (Beverley Vycital), 22 (Gregory Albertini).

Web Sites

Due to the changing nature of Internet links, PowerKids Press has
developed an online list of Web sites related to the subject of this book.
This site is updated regularly. Please use this link to access this list:
www.powerkidslinks.com/shtg/cat

Contents

What is a cat? 4

Wildcats 6

Domestic cats 8

A kitten is born 10

Growing up 12

Cat senses 14

Understanding cats 16

Many coats and colors 18

Choosing a pet cat 20

Caring for a cat 22

Glossary and Further Information 24

Index 24

What is a cat?

Cats that people keep as pets are known as **domestic cats**. They belong to a family of animals called **felids**. Some felids are much bigger than the domestic cat. These include lions and tigers.

▼ Cats are are very popular pets. They can make great companions.

Cats are meat-eating animals. Their bodies are well-suited to **hunting**. Cats can move quickly and quietly. They use their sharp claws and teeth to kill and eat their **prey**.

▲ Even a well-fed pet cat will hunt animals.

Wildcats

There are 36 different types of cat in the wild. Some are smaller than domestic cats. The European wildcat looks a lot like the domestic cat. It catches fish and hunts animals such as rabbits, mice, and insects.

▼ This European wildcat is found in Scotland.

The largest members of the cat family include tigers, lions, and leopards. Lions live together in groups, but most members of the cat family live alone.

▶ The Siberian tiger is the largest and heaviest type of tiger.

Cat Fact

The tiger is the biggest member of the cat family. Tigers can be over 10 ft. (3 m) long.

Domestic cats

People began keeping cats thousands of years ago. Cats would get rid of mice and rats in houses and farms. People also enjoyed having cats as companions.

Sometimes, domestic cats become homeless. They learn to survive without help from people. These cats and their **offspring** become half-wild. They are known as **feral cats**.

This Egyptian statue is thousands of years old. The ancient Egyptians admired cats for their beauty and hunting skill.

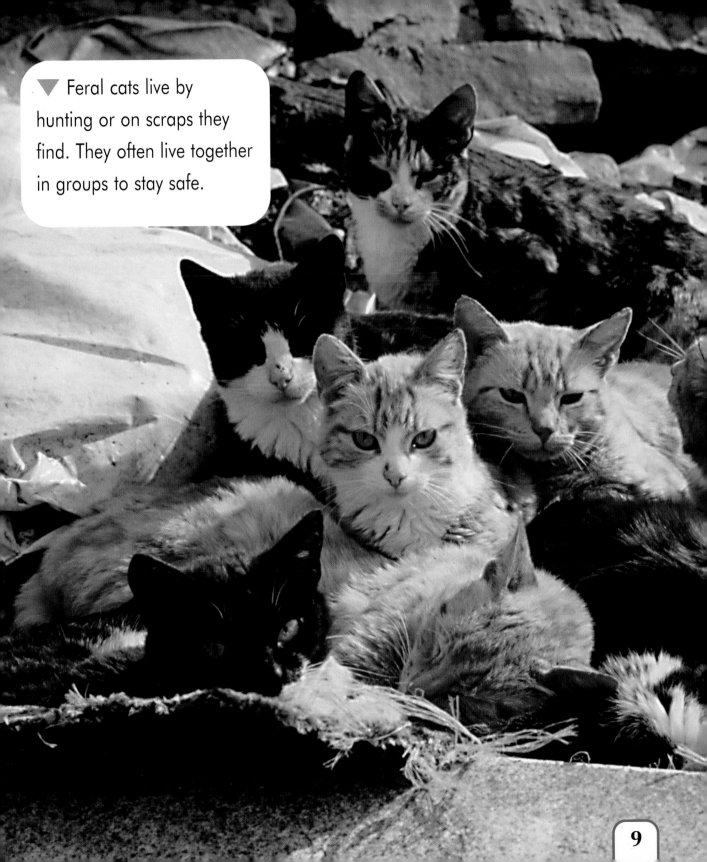

▼ Feral cats live by hunting or on scraps they find. They often live together in groups to stay safe.

A kitten is born

Mother cats usually have between three and five **kittens** in a **litter**. Kittens are born with their eyes shut. They sleep huddled together to stay warm. They open their eyes when they are about ten days old.

▼ Newborn kittens feed on their mother's milk.

Kittens start walking at three weeks.
At four weeks old, they begin to get
teeth and can start eating solid food.
At eight weeks old, a cat is ready to
leave its mother.

▲ A mother cat
uses her mouth to
move her kittens.

Growing up

Kittens are very playful. They love to play with each other. They will also play with toys, paper bags, and any pieces of string they find.

◀ Playing keeps a kitten fit. It is also good practice for hunting.

Cat Fact

The world's oldest cat lived for 38 years. Creme Puff lived in Texas and died in 1997.

A cat is grown-up when it is between ten and twelve months old. Cats usually live for between nine and fifteen years. Some live into their twenties.

▼ Cats spend lots of time sleeping. They usually sleep for about sixteen hours a day.

Cat senses

Cats have a strong sense of smell. They also have very good hearing and eyesight. Cats see better than people at night. Whiskers can help a cat to get around at night, too. The cat uses them to feel what is around it.

▲ Many pet cats like to go out hunting at night.

Cat Fact

A falling cat will twist its body so that it lands on its feet. It uses its great sense of balance to do this.

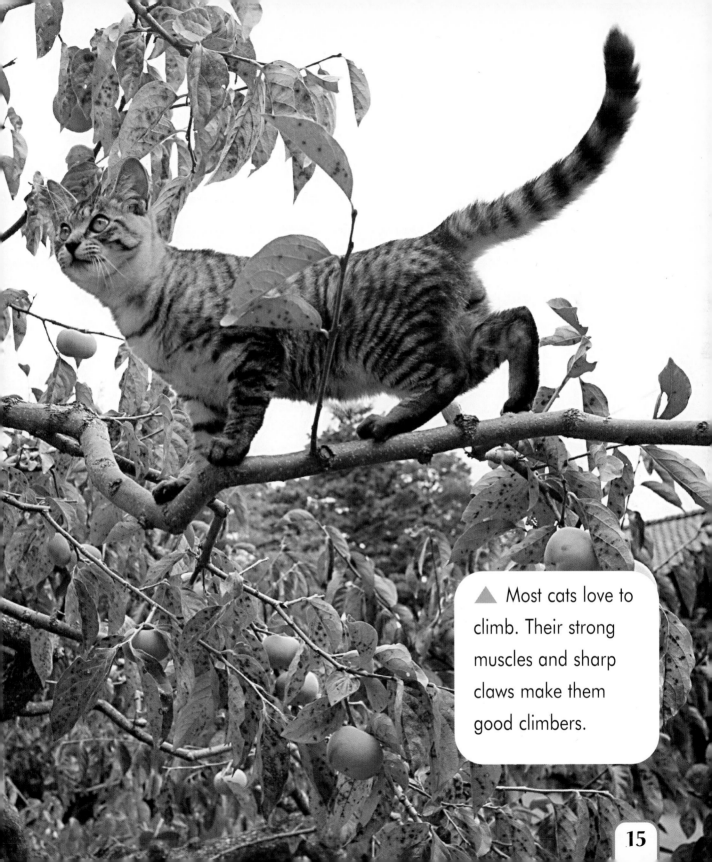

▲ Most cats love to climb. Their strong muscles and sharp claws make them good climbers.

Understanding cats

You can tell how a cat is feeling by watching it. A tail straight up means the cat is happy. An angry cat will flick his tail. A cat that is scared or ready to fight has a fluffed-up tail.

An angry cat may also hiss or growl. A happy cat usually makes a loud **purring** noise.

This cat is getting ready to scare off or attack an enemy.

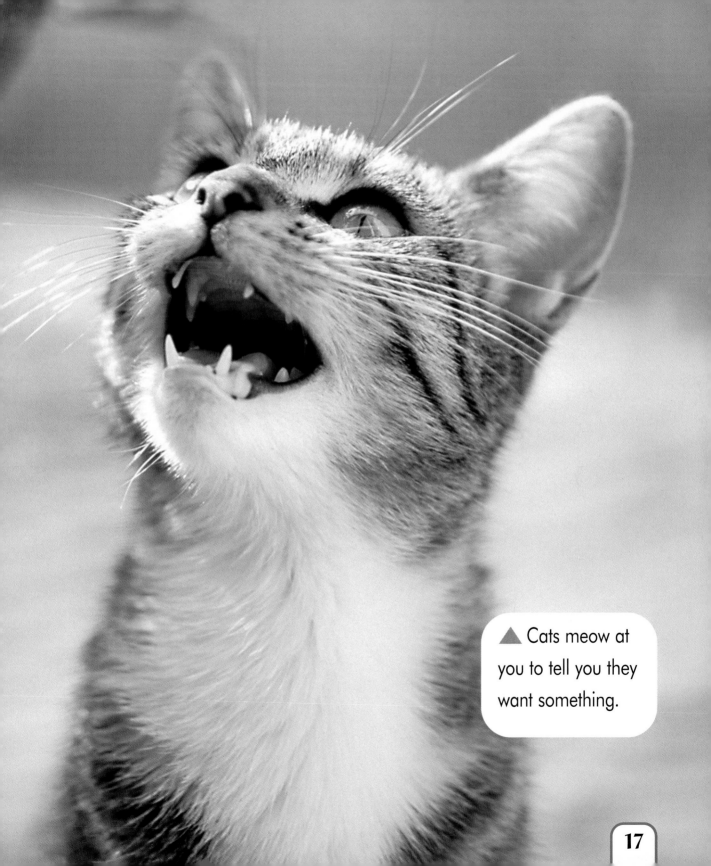

Cats meow at you to tell you they want something.

Many coats and colors

Cats can have many colors and markings. Special types of cat are called **breeds**. Most cats are a mixture of breeds.

▲ This Persian or Longhair cat has a flat face and long fur.

Some breeds have short, thick coats. Others have long fur. They may have different characters, too. Some breeds are more friendly than others.

Cat Fact

The Sphynx is a strange breed of cat. It has hardly any fur and no whiskers.

Siamese cats have dark faces, tails, and paws. They usually have a very loud meow.

Choosing a pet cat

If you want a pet cat, you must be sure that you can care for it properly. Then you can decide what kind of cat to have. Do you want a kitten? Would you prefer to give a home to an older cat?

◀ Animal shelters have many cats that need good homes.

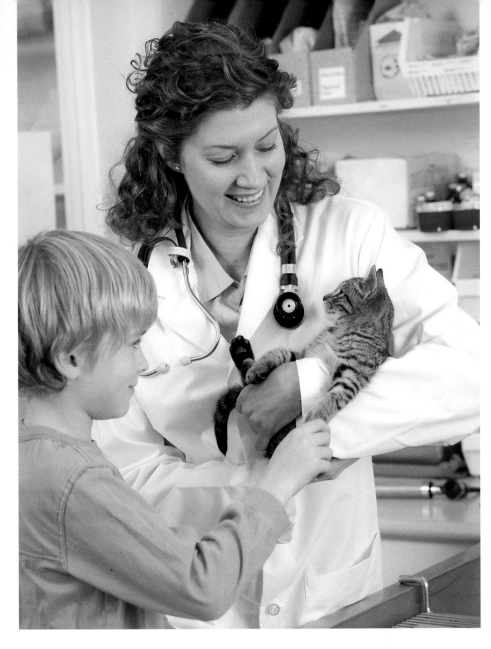

When you take your new cat to the vet, he or she will give it a health checkup.

A kitten will need to be **house trained**. This means teaching it to use a **litter tray**. Your pet will also need to see the vet for **vaccinations**. These will protect it from some diseases.

Caring for a cat

If you have a yard, a cat flap is a good idea.
This allows your cat to come and go
as it pleases. If your cat has to stay indoors,
you must make sure it gets exercise.

Your pet cat will love to play games with you. Playing will stop it from getting bored, and it is a great way of spending time with your cat.

◀ Playing with toys is good exercise for cats of all ages.

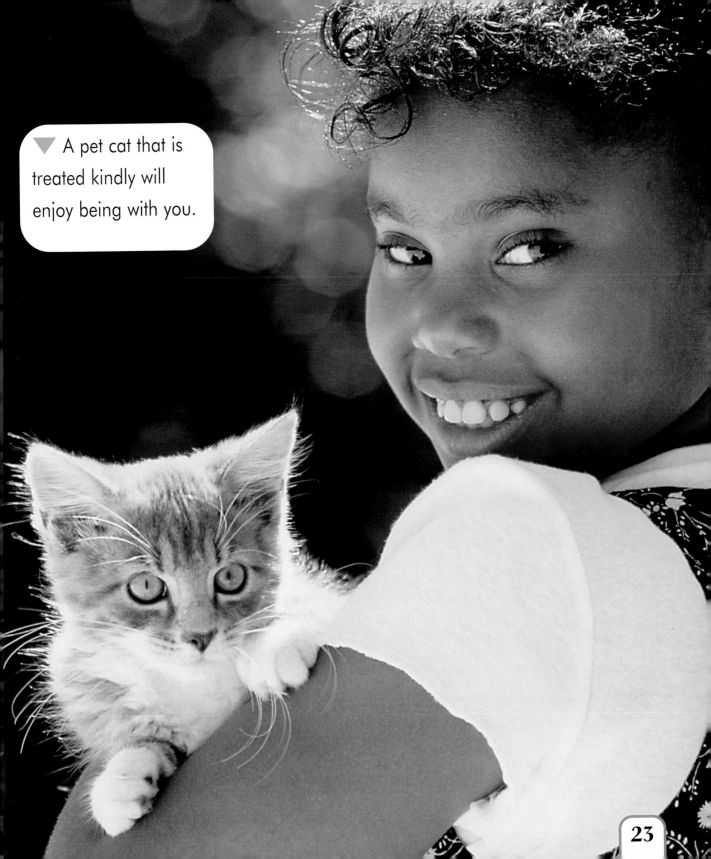

A pet cat that is treated kindly will enjoy being with you.

Glossary and Further Information

breed A special type of cat. Cats of the same breed are very similar. This is because their parents were of the same type or breed.

domestic cat Type of cat that lives with people and is kept as a pet.

felids Family of animals that includes domestic cats, lions, tigers, and wildcats.

feral cat A cat that is half wild. Feral cats are usually domestic cats that have lost their homes or have been born to homeless cats.

house trained A pet that has been trained to go to the bathroom outside or in a special place, such as a litter tray.

hunt To chase and kill an animal for food.

kitten A young cat.

litter The offspring, or young, born to an animal at one time.

litter tray A tray that an animal uses as its toilet.

offspring The young of an animal.

prey An animal that is hunted by another animal for food.

purring A vibrating sound that a cat makes in its throat. It usually does this when it is happy.

vaccination A shot that is given to protect people or animals against some serious diseases.

Books

A Pet's Life: Cats by Anita Ganeri (Heinemann, 2003)

Caring For Your Cat by Susan Ring (Topeka Bindery, 2003)

Index

balance, sense of 14

breeds 18–19
  Persian (Longhair) 18
  Siamese 19
  Sphynx 18

climbing 15

domestic cats 4, 5, 8, 18–23

European wildcat 6

exercise 22

eyesight 14

feeding 5, 10, 11

felids 4

feral cats 8, 9

hearing 14

house training 21

hunting 5, 6, 12, 14

kittens 10–11, 12

leopards 7

life span 13

lions 4, 7

litters 10

playing 12, 22

sleep 13

smell, sense of 14

sounds 16, 17, 19

tail 16

tigers 4, 7

vaccinations 21

vet 21

whiskers 14